DOUBLE FASTBACK®

R O M A N C E

C0-BLE-863

Chance of a Lifetime

Jennie Abbott

Fearon
Belmont, California

DOUBLE FASTBACK® ROMANCE Books

Chance of a Lifetime
Follow Your Dream
Good-Bye and Hello
Kiss and Make Up
Love in Bloom
A Love to Share
Never Too Late
No Secrets
The Road to Love
A Second Look

Cover illustrator: Terry Hoff

Copyright © 1987 by David S. Lake Publishers, 500 Harbor Boulevard, Belmont, California 94002. All rights reserved. No part of this book may be reproduced by any means, transmitted, or translated into a machine language without written permission from the publisher.

ISBN 0-8224-2382-0
Library of Congress Catalog Card Number: 86-81650
Printed in the United States of America
1. 9 8 7 6 5

"**H**ey, Vonnie!" Richie Montana called out as the pretty redhead walked up. "Nice day, huh?"

Yvonne Gordon, known as Vonnie to her friends, looked up at the bright blue sky. She smiled back at Richie. "Good thing it's a little cooler today," she answered. Then she began to help Richie unload some bags of cement from a truck.

1

Vonnie and Richie were construction laborers. This summer, they were working on the crew that was building the new Stonybrook Mall. The last few months had been long and hot. The humidity had matched the temperature nearly every day. Today, though, the cool morning air was welcome.

Ever since her childhood, Vonnie had dreamed of building skyscrapers. Her father, who had died seven years ago, had also been a laborer. When Vonnie was small, her father had driven her past a lot of construction sites. She had been thrilled by the tall, sleek girders that supported the buildings. Her real dream was to become an ironworker.

Vonnie had gotten into the laborers' union on her own merits. But she had found that becoming an ironworker was much more difficult.

Only ironworkers who were members of the ironworkers' union were allowed to put up steel frameworks for buildings. And to get into that union, a worker had to complete a three-year apprenticeship. Vonnie had applied for several of the training programs, but she had been turned down for all of them. She'd discovered that she needed help from someone in the ironworkers' union in order to get into an apprenticeship program.

Over the last few weeks, Vonnie had grown more and more unhappy. She had been working as a laborer for months now. She wanted some bigger challenges.

Today, Vonnie was so lost in her thoughts that she didn't notice Joe McGann walking past the truck. She nearly hit him with the sack of cement she was carrying before she saw him.

"Oh!" she said, startled. "Hi, Joe. How's it going?" Joe was the foreman of the iron-workers on this job.

Joe gave her a chilly smile. "I'll live, thanks," he replied, without stopping to say more.

Vonnie made a face at Joe's back as he passed her. But she never gave up trying to break through his icy reserve. She didn't think he could possibly dislike her as much as he seemed to. After all, she was one of the hardest workers on the site. But Joe acted as if he'd rather have Bugs Bunny working with him than a woman.

Then Vonnie turned again, and she caught Richie's eye. He smiled as though he knew how she must feel. Then he shrugged his shoulders as if to say, "Who knows? Maybe someday Joe will actually treat you like a human being."

Sometimes Vonnie wondered how she'd have survived this job if it hadn't been for Richie. She remembered her first day on the project.

She had liked Richie right from the start. He was very friendly and easygoing. And he had shown Vonnie all around the construction site. He had gentle brown eyes and tousled dark brown hair. Vonnie figured he probably combed his hair only about every two days.

That afternoon, Richie had introduced Vonnie to Joe. Joe had shaken her hand as if he were meeting someone who had the plague. His first words to her had been,

"Don't expect any special favors around here. This is a tough job for tough people." With that, he had walked away.

Richie had explained then that Joe was kind of old-fashioned.

"Old-fashioned!" Vonnie had repeated. "Why? He can't be much older than I am!"

"He's just not used to having women around on the job," Richie had answered. "But he's a nice guy. Really. You'll get used to him."

"But will *he* get used to *me*?" Vonnie had asked.

"Depends," Richie had said.

"On what?" Vonnie had wondered.

"Oh, on a few things," Richie had replied. "Like how well you know your job. And how well you follow the safety rules." Then Richie had nodded. "Yeah, Joe's a real stickler when it comes to safety. There are never any accidents when he's the foreman. Other foremen aren't so careful."

"What do you mean?" Vonnie had asked.

"Oh, some foremen don't pay much attention to building codes and safety codes," Richie had explained. "Remember that crane that fell over on the woman at the Grovewood site?"

Vonnie remembered it well. "That was awful," she had answered.

"It sure was," Richie had agreed. "And she got a ten-million-dollar settlement from the construction firm. That kind of thing would never happen with Joe around. He's careful—not because of the money, but because he cares about his men."

"*And* women?" Vonnie had asked with raised eyebrows.

A slow grin had spread over Richie's face. "Yes," he had answered. "Joe really cares about everyone he's responsible for."

That had been the end of that conversation. As the summer passed, Joe McGann had continued to avoid Vonnie. But to Richie, it had never mattered that Vonnie was a woman—on the job, that is. He had asked Vonnie out only three days after he had met her. And Vonnie still went bowling with Richie every week. But she made sure they stayed "just friends." She didn't want people to think she might be using a fellow worker to further her career.

As Vonnie threw another bag of cement onto a hand truck, she caught sight of Joe again. He was up on the third floor of the building nearest her. He and another ironworker were bending over to lift a large steel plate. As she watched the sunlight glisten off the steel, Vonnie felt a pang of envy flow through her. That was the type of work she longed to do. And if given the chance, she felt sure she could do it.

Joe had been right when he'd said that the job would be tough. Throughout the hot summer months, Vonnie had put in long hours of hard, physical work. But she had loved every minute of it. And it had paid off. Vonnie had steadily built up her strength. Now she could do her job without ever having to stop to catch her breath.

Vonnie reached down for the last sack of cement on the truck. "Yes," she said to herself, "I'm strong enough for this work.

Even Joe McGann has to agree with that. But am I strong enough to climb any higher?"

By late afternoon, the weather had turned hot and sticky. Vonnie and Richie had been assigned to cleanup duty—sweeping the steel decks before the concrete for the floors was poured.

Vonnie pushed her broom, gathering a pile of scrap rubber, paper, and some discarded nuts and bolts. "I never thought that neatness would matter on a job like this," she said.

Richie grinned as he swept the deck alongside her. He'd taken off his shirt, revealing the lean muscles of his tanned chest and shoulders. He had a bright red bandana tied around his neck. "This is the kind of job I like," he said contentedly.

Vonnie glanced at him. "Richie, don't you ever get tired of just pushing a broom?" she asked.

"There are worse jobs," he answered.

Just then someone shouted, "Hey, Vonnie!" She looked up to see one of the ironworkers leaning around a girder. "Did you sweep up a screwdriver? I think I left one over there."

"No," Vonnie called back, looking around. Then she spotted the screwdriver a little farther away. "Wait a minute," she yelled over to the worker.

She walked over and bent to pick up the screwdriver. But when she grabbed it, it wouldn't budge. Vonnie tugged, but the screwdriver stayed firmly attached to the steel deck. Behind her, she could hear the sounds of laughter.

Richie walked over to her. "It's an old joke," he explained. "Somebody welds the screwdriver to the deck. Then an iron-worker asks a new worker to pick it up."

"Right," said Vonnie, her face turning red and hot. "Really funny."

To make things worse, Joe McGann appeared on the deck just then. He was frowning and his gray eyes looked as cold and hard as steel. "Don't you clowns have enough work to keep you busy?" he barked. "We've got to make sure this deck is welded down before we pour the concrete."

The ironworkers rushed away. "And Montana," Joe went on, looking over at

Richie, "according to the safety code, you should be wearing a shirt." He glanced briefly at Vonnie and walked away.

Richie put his shirt back on. "Joe really does care about safety," he remarked.

The picture of Joe McGann walking away stayed in Vonnie's mind all through the ride home after work. He had seemed so angry. It disturbed her that a foreman, whose strength and position she admired, may have thought she had been playing around on the job.

That evening at the bowling alley, Vonnie couldn't keep her mind on the game. Richie was way ahead—which was not the way their games usually went. Although he loved to bowl, Richie never practiced. "It's just a game," he'd say. "Why get bent out of shape over it?"

She was shaken out of her thoughts by Richie's voice. "Hey, it's your turn," he reminded her.

"Oh," Vonnie responded. "Sorry." She got up to get her ball.

"Are you still stewing over what happened today?" Richie asked. "That screwdriver thing? Come on, Vonnie, it was just a joke. It happens to everybody who's new on the job." He grinned. "When I started, the guys had me wandering around for half an hour looking for a left-handed monkey wrench. It was Joe who finally told me that it was a joke. I thought he was going to explode laughing."

"He wasn't laughing today," Vonnie said.

"So what's the problem?" Richie asked. "Are you upset because the ironworkers laughed or because Joe didn't? He doesn't have much to laugh about right now. We're supposed to be pouring concrete tomorrow night. And the deck on the third floor isn't even finished yet." Then Richie shook his head. "Look, I don't want to stay here and talk about work. What do you say we leave?" he suggested.

"But the game!" Vonnie said.

Richie shrugged. "Let's forget it," he said.

After paying for their games, Richie and Vonnie walked through the bowling alley to the parking lot. The evening air felt warm and pleasant.

They got into Richie's car. "Why don't we go over to Stonybrook Park and look at the brook?" Richie asked.

Vonnie smiled. The park, though in the middle of town, was one of her favorite places. With its pine trees, winding dirt paths, and grass-covered hills, it seemed like a place miles away from a bustling city.

Vonnie's thoughts were scattered during the ride to the park. Her mind went back and forth between work that day and the way she'd acted at the bowling alley. She looked forward to the peacefulness of the park.

"Why so quiet?" Richie asked after a few moments.

"Oh, no reason, really," Vonnie answered. "I guess I just have a lot on my mind."

Richie parked, and they got out of the car. Even though the sun had gone down, there was a fair amount of light from the moon. Vonnie found a big rock on top of a hill and sat down, gazing at the wandering brook.

Richie stood beside her. He gently ran his fingers through her short, curly red-blond hair.

"I don't know what you're worrying about, Vonnie," he said. "You're doing fine on the job. Everybody likes you. . . ." He stopped for a moment. "And you know *I* like you."

Vonnie looked up to see him give her a lopsided smile. She didn't know what to say. Sure, she *liked* Richie. But sometimes she felt that Richie liked her as more than a friend. Did sharing good times and being comfortable with someone mean that you were in love? Vonnie didn't know.

Richie leaned over and brushed her lips with a brief kiss. He sat down beside Vonnie and put his arm around her. She rested her head on his shoulder and looked at the brook. They sat there, lost in their own thoughts, until the sky clouded over and it became too dark to see anymore.

The next day at work was the busiest Vonnie had seen since she'd started. "They're pouring the concrete tonight," Richie explained. "The last-minute preparations are always a little wild. Everything has to be perfect when the concrete goes down. Otherwise, the whole schedule for the building will get fouled up."

All the laborers spent the day buzzing around the construction site, moving supplies and equipment out of the way. Vonnie's job was to work with a gang cleaning up after workers from the other unions. Plumbers, steamfitters, and electricians were working frantically. All the pipes for water, heat, and wires had to be laid down before the cement flooring was poured.

The ironworkers were busy, too. To build each floor, the concrete would be poured over steel deck plates. But first, each deck plate had to be welded to girders, and the ironworkers had to check all the welds.

Today it was Vonnie's turn to pick up the lunch order for her work gang. As she walked up the stairs with the box of sandwiches and sodas that had been ordered, she ran into Joe McGann.

"Hi, Joe," Vonnie said.

But Joe walked right past her. He didn't even look up from the clipboard he was holding.

"Sure Joe, you have a nice day, too," Vonnie muttered sarcastically. She stomped up the stairs.

When quitting time finally came around, she was ready for it. But as she headed down to the trailers to wash up, Richie stopped her.

"Vonnie, the boss needs somebody to work a little overtime," Richie told her. "One of the pipe crews on the third floor left a mess, and it's got to be cleaned up. I can't stay late tonight. But I thought you might want the extra pay."

"OK," Vonnie said. "Tell him I'll do the job."

"Um, I know I usually give you a lift home," Richie started. "But if you're working late—"

"It's OK," Vonnie cut in. "I can take a bus home." She quickly grabbed a broom from the supply shed. "Now where am I supposed to go?"

Richie gave her the directions, and Vonnie marched up the stairs with the broom over her shoulder.

The mess wasn't really that big. It took her just a few minutes to clean it up. But by the time Vonnie was finished, everyone else had gone home.

She was getting ready to leave when all of a sudden, one of the deck plates began sagging under her feet.

Vonnie stepped back, watching the plate wobble. Then she looked at the edges. They weren't welded down. The whole plate was loose!

"Oh, no," Vonnie muttered. She picked up her broom and rushed down the stairs toward the ironworkers' trailer.

Joe McGann was just outside, locking up.

"Boy, am I glad you're still around!" Vonnie exclaimed.

Joe looked a little annoyed as he turned to her. Vonnie noticed that he still had the clipboard under his arm. "What is it?" he demanded.

When he heard Vonnie's story, Joe's expression went from annoyance to dismay. "How did that get past us?" he asked, shuffling through the pages on his clipboard. "It's too late to call a crew back. They're supposed to be pouring concrete up there in a little while."

He unlocked the door to the supply shed and rushed inside. "I'll have to weld it down myself—if I can get the equipment up there in time," Joe said.

"I'll help," Vonnie called through the open door.

Joe's face popped back into the doorway. "You'll what?" he asked, sounding surprised.

"I'll help," she repeated.

"But it's not your job," Joe replied. He pushed a welding torch, a mask, and two gas tanks out of the supply shed.

"I can carry some of this stuff," Vonnie said. "And helping to get this building done *is* my job."

"I guess beggars can't be choosers," Joe mumbled. His face took on a hardened look again. Then he softened. "No. I'm glad you're here to help, Yvonne," he admitted.

Together, they carried the welding equipment up to the third floor. "Hold these for a second," Joe said, giving Vonnie what looked like a handful of metal spaghetti. He put on his welder's mask.

"These are welder's rods, aren't they?" she asked, looking at the metal pieces in her hands.

"Yes," Joe replied. "You melt them with the torch and use them as solder. The solder holds the deck plates together." He stopped for a second. "I guess you've never handled a torch before."

"No," Vonnie said.

"Here," Joe said, tossing her a pair of heavy goggles. "Put these on. And *don't look at the flame on the torch!*"

He hooked up the gas feeds, flipped the visor down on his mask, and then lit the torch. Even through the dark goggles, Vonnie could see the blazing flame.

Joe leaned over the edge of the loose plate. "I'm going to have to shift this," he said, his voice muffled by the mask.

Vonnie pulled the heavy work gloves from her belt, slipped them on, and went to the other side of the plate. Working together, she and Joe moved it into position.

"You're smart and strong," Joe said. "I have to admit that I'm surprised." He bent over and got down to the job of working his way around the plate. He welded it to the girders and to the other plates around it.

Vonnie watched, fascinated. Welding rods dribbled away as Joe placed them in the white-hot tip of flame at the end of the torch.

After ten minutes, Joe cut the flame and flipped up the visor. "Almost done," he said. "It's not beautiful, but it'll hold." Then he grinned up at Vonnie. "What do people call you? Is it Vonnie?" he asked.

"Most people," Vonnie answered.

"Well, Vonnie, how would you like to put on the finishing touch?" Joe asked.

"Me?" Vonnie asked, surprised.

"Sure," Joe replied. He pulled off his mask and handed it to Vonnie. "Wear this and be careful," he told her. "I'll wear your goggles. That'll be safe."

Vonnie put on the mask and a pair of heavy gloves. Then Joe showed her how to direct the flame on the torch. "Just push a little bit of the rod into the flame," he instructed. "That's right . . . and move the torch along. . . ." He brought his hand down on her wrist. Vonnie felt that somehow his touch gave her hands more confidence.

"All done," Joe stated after a few minutes.

Vonnie snapped off the torch, flipped up the visor, and smiled at Joe. For the first time, she noticed the flecks of red in his short brown hair, and how red his carefully trimmed mustache was.

Joe smiled back. "Thanks for the help, Vonnie," he said. "I owe you for this."

They carried the equipment back to the supply shed. Vonnie headed off to clean up. Then she stopped. Everything would be locked up at this hour. She'd just have to stay grubby for the ride home on the bus.

She stood at the bus stop, looking at her watch and wondering when the bus would come. Then a car pulled up.

"Vonnie. *Vonnie!*" It was Joe, calling to her through his car window. "Need a lift?"

Vonnie hesitated before deciding to accept Joe's offer. But as grimy as she felt, getting a ride would be better than waiting forever for the bus. She nodded to Joe and then stepped into the car.

Vonnie felt a little embarrassed as she settled into the car seat. "I'm a mess," she said, after telling him where she lived. "I just want to get home and clean up."

"Oh?" asked Joe. "Something big tonight? I hope I didn't keep you."

"No," she answered, smiling. "Unless you count being clean as something big."

They chatted some more. Vonnie was surprised to discover that Joe *could* talk when he wanted to.

Then, as they neared Vonnie's street, Joe glanced at her and said, "I was thinking. There's a concert at Stonybrook Park tonight. Want to go?"

For a second, Vonnie didn't know what to say. Then, before she could think any further, she heard herself saying, "Sure."

Joe smiled. "I'll get ready, pick up a bite for us to eat, and come back for you at

7:30," he suggested. "Will that give you enough time?"

"That should be fine," Vonnie said as she got out of the car.

"See you then," Joe called as he pulled away.

Vonnie ran into the house, and then froze by the mirror in the hallway. "Oh, no!" she cried. "My hair!"

Her hard hat had matted down her curls. Vonnie dashed for the bathroom. "This is a job for a shower and my blow-drier," she decided. "I just hope I'll be ready in time."

The following Monday, Vonnie went shopping after work with her friend Dawn.

"Come on, tell!" Dawn demanded. "You said one of the bosses from work asked you out. Who was it? *And what happened?*"

"Well, it was Joe McGann," Vonnie began.

"I thought he didn't like you!" said Dawn.

"So did I. But he didn't act that way when we went out," Vonnie said. "He picked up sandwiches and German potato salad from Muller's deli. We had a picnic in the park. And the outdoor concert was wonderful." Her eyes shone. "It was really fun!"

"I thought it rained that evening," Dawn remembered.

"It did—but not until after the concert," Vonnie said. "Joe just scooped up the blanket we were sitting on and held it over us while we ran. We laughed all the way to the car."

"Sounds great," Dawn said enviously.

"Yeah," Vonnie answered slowly. "It was . . . different."

"Different from bowling, you mean," Dawn said with a sly smile. "So how has Joe acted since then?"

Vonnie lowered her eyes. "The next day at work, he was businesslike again," she answered. She looked up at Dawn. "He said that's the way it will have to be. And he's right. I don't want to look like the teacher's pet—or a foreman's pet. But it was rough to have him be so nice in the evening and so distant the next day."

For the next couple of days, Vonnie hardly had a chance to talk with Joe. Every time she saw him, he was with a bunch of ironworkers, setting up another part of the job.

The laborers were pretty busy, too, moving equipment around. "Hey, Vonnie," Richie called as he pushed a heavy cart full of tools. "Hope you won't be too tired for bowling tonight."

Bowling! Vonnie had almost forgotten their bowling date.

That evening at the bowling alley, Vonnie almost wished that she *had* forgotten about the date. Once again, she couldn't keep her mind on the game or on what Richie was saying. She just didn't feel very interested. Finally, she wound up keeping score. Richie bowled with another guy, a laborer from the job who often hung around the bowling alley.

As they left the alley and walked through the parking lot to the car, Richie turned to look at Vonnie. "I think we'd better talk," he said. "Something's bothering you, Vonnie. Your game has been lousy two weeks in a row. What's wrong?"

"It's hard to tell you, Richie," Vonnie began. "I don't know. . . ." She took a deep breath. Then she continued. "Until the last two weeks, we've usually had a good time bowling. It's just that—well, everything is always the same," she finally blurted out. "You don't seem to like to do anything different."

Richie looked thoughtful. "Yeah," he said in a quiet voice. "I know that when you went out with Joe, you went someplace different—to a concert or something. We should try a change, too. Maybe a movie or something."

"Maybe," Vonnie said, surprised that Richie knew about her date.

They got into the car, and he drove her home in silence.

Over the next couple of days at work, Vonnie realized that word really had gotten out about her date with Joe. He must have told at least one person. Several times, she overheard ironworkers kidding him about it.

Once, while she was helping run the elevator, a gang of workers came aboard—followed by Joe. He didn't notice Vonnie until she started ringing the bell that signaled the hoist operator as to what floor she wanted.

"Hey, Joe," said one of the guys, laughing. "You want us to get off at the next floor and—uh—leave you alone?"

Joe wasn't smiling when he answered. "Listen up, you comedians," he ordered, his voice sounding gruff and businesslike. "I want to see you on the fourth deck, welding those panels in. And it would be nice if you kept your minds on the job this time. Don't forget the panel you missed on the third deck."

The elevator reached the fourth level and he stomped out the door. The crew followed quietly. Vonnie signaled to be returned to ground level. After seeing the look on Joe's face, she was sure he would never even talk to her again.

It was Richie's turn to get lunches that day. He showed up beside her at noon with a box of food in his hands and a grin on his face. "You looked a little down today," he said. "So besides the ham on rye, I picked up your favorite." He dug down through the sandwiches and came up with a box of animal crackers.

Vonnie had to laugh. Richie handed her a soda and said, "I've got to go feed the rest of the troops. I'll see you later."

She watched him run along the new concrete floor, the box of food on his shoulder. Then she realized someone was beside her. She turned to see Joe standing there.

For once, he didn't have his clipboard. He was carrying a sandwich. And he looked a little worried. "Vonnie, I'm sorry I haven't had much time to talk to you lately," he said. Then he spotted the package in her hand. "Animal crackers?" he asked.

"That's right," she said. "Want a lion or a tiger?"

"What I could use right now is the ring-master," Joe replied. "It's been like a circus up there with the guys. Especially with all the kidding." He took a deep breath. "And that's what I wanted to talk about," he said.

Vonnie glanced over at him. "Here comes the bad news," she thought.

"There's a dance contest at the Mirror One Club Friday night," Joe said. "Would you like to go?"

Vonnie stared at him in surprise. "Are you crazy?" she asked.

Joe smiled and shrugged. "If I'm going to get teased, I'd better make sure it's worth it," he said. "And I'd like to go with you. So what do you say?"

Vonnie found herself smiling, too. "I may be just as crazy as you are," she answered. "I'll say yes."

When Friday night came, Vonnie had a struggle deciding what to wear. She was used to wearing work clothes around Joe. It felt strange to think of getting dressed up to be with him. She certainly didn't want him to think she was dressing up to impress him.

Yet Mirror One was supposed to be a classy club. And if Joe happened to think she looked nice . . . well, she *had* enjoyed their evening at the park.

Vonnie finally decided on her white mini-skirt with the slit, a pale pink lace tank top, and white heels. Her new long pink jacket would finish off the look. She dressed quickly and then glanced at the mirror, satisfied.

She was running a comb through her curls when she heard Joe ring the doorbell. Vonnie thought he looked terrific in his gray slacks, sports jacket, shirt, and tie. Hoping she hadn't stared too long, she invited him in.

Joe stepped through the doorway and looked at Vonnie admiringly. "You look great," he told her. "Can this be the same woman who helped me weld down a deck plate in her old Levi's?"

Vonnie just smiled. "Ready to go?" she asked.

They got into Joe's silver Camaro and headed for the club. Vonnie felt a bit nervous as they drove off. She didn't know what to expect from Joe. He had seemed friendly enough when he had asked her out the other day. But she couldn't forget the irritated look on his face when the guys at work had teased him.

After a few minutes, Vonnie felt her nervousness start to fade. Once again, away from the job, Joe was like a different person. Smiling and full of jokes, he kept up a steady conversation.

"You know," Vonnie said as they neared the club, "you should put down your clipboard more often."

"What do you mean?" Joe asked, sounding a little confused.

"It's just that you're less serious—and a lot more fun—without it," Vonnie answered.

"Come on," Joe protested. "I kid around with the guys at work." Then he glanced over at her. "Oh. I get it," he said. "I don't joke much around you." He sighed. "It isn't easy, you know," he pointed out. "First, it was getting used to having a woman on the job. And now . . ." He smiled at Vonnie. "Now, it's figuring out what to do about a hardworking woman who wants to build buildings."

They pulled up in front of Mirror One. "But tonight, we can forget about all that," Joe went on. "All we have to think about now is dancing, right?"

"I guess so," Vonnie replied, hoping he was right.

After they'd been there awhile, Vonnie was amazed at how much she was enjoying herself. Joe had still more surprises for her. He was a fantastic dancer! As she watched him move gracefully to the music, she wished the guys on the job could see them now. Joe could really be a lot of fun.

They danced with energy, and the evening flew by. They didn't win the first prize. But they were among the top ten dancers.

"You should have gotten a better partner," Vonnie said as they left. "You could have gone right to the finals."

"No way," Joe said. He gave her a gentle smile as he shook his head. "I had the only partner I wanted."

Tired, Vonnie and Joe got into the car and headed back to Vonnie's. The route that Joe chose took them right past the construction site. As they passed it, Vonnie saw the tall, gaunt girders rising up against the face of the full moon.

"The mall will really be something when it's finished," Vonnie remarked.

"Yeah, you get a special feeling inside when you see a building you worked on get finished," Joe agreed. "But there's a bad side, too," he said. He looked a little sad. "When the job's over, the crew breaks up. Laborers and ironworkers move on to other jobs. You know you might never see them again. A lot of times, I miss some of the guys."

He pulled the car over to the side of the road and parked. "I've watched you work, Vonnie," he said. "And I've heard about how ambitious you are. You won't be satisfied staying a laborer for the rest of your life. It sounds as if you want to go further." He reached into the glove compartment and brought out some folded papers.

"What are these?" Vonnie asked.

Joe handed her the papers. "Look and see," he told her. Then he switched on the overhead light.

Vonnie opened the papers and her eyes widened. "It's an application form for an ironworker's apprenticeship," she said. "But what are these extra sheets?" She paged through them. "Recommendations!" she exclaimed. "From half the ironworkers on the site!"

"I knew that you were interested in an apprenticeship," Joe said. "But you don't have much chance of getting one around this area unless union members back you up. I'd happily stand up for you. But I don't think my recommendation would do you much good. People don't think I'm exactly impartial toward you. So I got the other guys to notice what kind of a worker you are. And once they did, they had to agree that you've got what it takes."

Vonnie was still staring a little dazedly at the papers.

"You'd have a good chance now, if you put in another application," Joe said.

"I . . . I—" Somehow, Vonnie's voice didn't seem to be working. Tears began to form in her eyes and run down her cheeks.

Joe's face was stricken as he leaned over and put his arm around her. "Oh, Vonnie! I didn't mean to upset you," he said. "I'm sorry."

"Don't be silly," Vonnie said, finally getting control of her voice. "Joe, I want . . ." She looked up, and a second later she was kissing him.

"Vonnie," Joe whispered.

Although they drove home in silence, Vonnie had never felt so close to anyone in her life. When they pulled up in front of her apartment building, Joe leaned over and gave her another kiss. "Thanks, Vonnie," he said. "This has been a great evening."

"I should be thanking you," Vonnie said, taking his hand and squeezing it. "When you asked me out, I wasn't sure how the night would turn out. But it was perfect."

Vonnie picked up the application and papers and reached out to open the door. Joe jumped out and walked around the car to meet her. Hand in hand, they walked up the path to her apartment.

When they got to her door, Joe kissed her once again. "I hate to see this evening end," he said.

"Oh, so do I," Vonnie agreed. "But I guess I'll see you on Monday. I suppose it'll be back to business-as-usual then."

Joe gave her a half-smile. "I imagine so," he said. "But you've got to understand. It's not easy being a foreman."

"I guess not," Vonnie said. She held up the application papers. "But you've done something really special for me, Joe. Thanks. And good night."

Vonnie went inside. She stood by the window and watched as Joe walked to his car and drove away. She still couldn't believe how lucky she was. She took one more look at the application. She knew she was holding the chance of a lifetime in her hands.

Vonnie tried to calm down, but she couldn't stop thinking about Joe and all he had done for her. She knew this was her chance to become an ironworker. At last her dream was going to come true.

Suddenly she thought about Richie. How was she going to tell him about this? What would it do to their friendship?

Vonnie didn't get much sleep that weekend. She couldn't stop thinking about her apprenticeship application. She still hadn't decided what she would say to Richie when she dragged herself into work Monday morning.

Luckily, there wasn't much heavy work going on. She was put on a sweeping crew on the ground floor. "Thank goodness Richie isn't working down here today," she thought.

Later, though, Richie came around to take lunch orders. And just as he was taking Vonnie's, an ironworker happened to walk by.

"Hey, Gordon," the man called out. "I hear you may be joining us after a while. McGann really went to bat for you. He even got me to sign a letter recommending you for an apprenticeship!" Then the guy walked off. Richie stood there staring at Vonnie. "Vonnie, what's he talking about?" he finally asked.

Vonnie looked down at the cement floor, trying to find the right words. Finally, she decided on the straight truth.

"Joe McGann was impressed with the way I helped fasten down a loose deck plate," she said. "I guess he'd heard that I wanted to be an ironworker. So he went around to get some help for my application for an apprenticeship." Then she looked up, almost afraid of what she would see. But Richie actually started laughing.

"Poor Joe," he chuckled.

"What do you mean, 'poor Joe'?" she asked.

"If he thought he got teased for going out with you, just wait till the kidding starts about this!" he said. He began imitating one of the laborers. "Hey, Joe!" he teased. "What's Vonnie got that I don't have? Or maybe I'm just not pretty enough for the job?"

"It's not that way at all!" Vonnie said, her face flaming. "You can't believe that."

Richie's face got serious. "I don't, Vonnie," he said. "But that's because I know you. All the time we've worked together, you've never tried to use me to get a softer job. Even though you knew I'd do anything for you."

Vonnie opened her mouth to speak, but Richie raised his hand to stop her. "Look, don't worry about me," he said. "But some of the other guys on the job don't know you very well. And they're going to have their say. To Joe—and to you. So you'd better be ready for it."

"Oh, Richie," Vonnie sighed. "You've always been a good friend."

Richie's lopsided smile came back. "Yeah," he said, "and I guess that's about the way it's going to be, too." Then his eyes softened. "Joe must think you're really special to go through all of this for you," he said, shaking his head. "I should have guessed it from the way he looks at you. And the way you've been looking at him lately."

"Richie, I never meant . . ." Vonnie began.

Richie's smile was gentle. "You don't need to say anything, Vonnie," he told her. "I enjoy being a laborer. But I know you want to do more." He put his hand on her shoulder and squeezed gently. "So, good luck." Then he walked away.

Vonnie stood leaning on her broom, watching him go. Her mind was a whirl of thoughts. Poor, easygoing Richie! And poor Joe! When he had given her those papers, she hadn't realized how it would look to the ironworkers—and to the other people on the job. He was really going through a lot to do this favor for her.

Then another thought came into her head. Would Joe really take all this trouble (and all the ribbing he'd be sure to get) just because he thought Vonnie deserved a better job? Or could he be doing it just because he liked her?

When quitting time finally came around, Vonnie was exhausted. It wasn't the work that was tiring. Her body automatically took care of the job. It was all the thinking she'd been doing that had tired her out. Still deep in thought, she headed for the bus stop and took the next bus home.

As soon as she got home, Vonnie took a quick shower. Then she put on a summery white sweater, yellow pants, and sandals. She sat on her bed, wondering about Joe's reasons for helping her out. Suddenly, she couldn't stand it anymore. She grabbed the phone book, looked up Joe's number, and dialed.

Joe answered in his gruff, "business" voice. But his tone changed when he realized who was calling. "What can I do for you, Vonnie?" he asked.

"I'd like to talk about the apprenticeship application," she said. "It sounded pretty good to me until some of the guys started kidding me about it today."

"Well, you know how the guys are," Joe pointed out. "They always need something to laugh about. What's the problem?"

"I can handle the teasing," Vonnie answered. "But I thought you must be getting it even worse. And that made me wonder why you're doing all of this for me."

"I like the way you've been working," Joe said, a little too quickly.

"That's not what the guys are saying," Vonnie cut in. "And I was wondering if there was . . . more."

She could hear Joe's heavy sigh. "Look, Vonnie," he said sternly. "That's not the way I do things. You're a hard worker. And on the merits of your work I thought you had the potential for more demanding jobs." Then he stopped for a moment. "I'm surprised you even had to ask me something like that," he said, sounding hurt.

Then Vonnie spoke up. "But, Joe—"

Abruptly, Joe broke in. "Look. Maybe we shouldn't be talking about this over the phone. Would you mind if I came over after I wash up a bit?"

"That would be fine, Joe," Vonnie replied.

After she hung up, Vonnie read the recommendations once again. "Hardworking," "Cheerful," "Ready to give that little extra on the job," they said.

"This isn't just Joe talking," she realized. "These really are the opinions of the guys."

Once again she read over what Joe'd written. "Recommended for an ironworker's apprenticeship program." How could she include that one after the way she had just insulted him?

Vonnie sighed. Her father had always talked about "paying dues." Was giving up her friendship with Joe the "dues" she'd have to pay to become an ironworker? Vonnie didn't want to do that.

Joe was a special guy—warm, friendly, and funny, too. She remembered the way he'd laughed in the rain at the park. But he was also a tough, all-business foreman who could chew out a crew of rugged iron-workers. Vonnie had to admit that she admired both sides of him.

Joe appeared at her door a half hour later. Vonnie had never before seen him look unsure of himself. He seemed even more ill at ease when he went into the living room and saw her application on the coffee table.

"I've been trying to decide whether to send it in," Vonnie explained.

"Trying to decide!" Joe sputtered. "Are you crazy?" He was quiet for a second. Then he spoke again, a little less excitedly.

"If I were in your shoes, I wouldn't even think twice," he said.

"Well, *I'm* in my shoes," Vonnie replied. "And I've thought more than twice about it."

"If you're worrying about what the guys will say, you should reread those recommendations," Joe said. "The guys all think you'll be a great ironworker."

"And what about you?" Vonnie asked.

"I think you should send it in," Joe said.

"Are you talking as a foreman?" she asked. "Or as a friend?"

Joe stared down and fiddled with the papers. Then he looked up again. "As both, I suppose," he answered. "You've impressed me since the first time you came on the site."

"What?" asked Vonnie, her voice rising. "I thought you didn't like me! That you were old-fashioned about having women on the job."

"I'll admit that I didn't think women were tough enough for the work," Joe said. "But that first day, you changed my mind. I was downright unfriendly, but you kept your cool. And you went out and did a full day's work. I admired that. If I'd known about your applications then, I'd have written a recommendation right away." Then he looked down again. "Now I know you and like you, too," he said quietly.

"But now people think you're helping me *just* because you like me," Vonnie said. "They'll say I'm using you to get ahead."

Joe shrugged. "As I always say," he replied, "it's not easy being a foreman." He smiled. "And this situation can't be easy for you, either. But if you do a good job . . ."

". . . and stay businesslike," Vonnie laughed.

Joe smiled and nodded. "This ordeal will be history almost before you know it," he said. "If you were tough enough to put up with me being unfriendly, you can live through some stupid jokes."

"Paying my dues," Vonnie murmured.

"Right," said Joe. "So what do you say?"

"I say we should go out and mail these right away," Vonnie said, ruffling through the papers. "Just wait a second. I want to put your recommendation right on top."

They left Vonnie's apartment and walked to the mailbox, two blocks away. After mailing the packet, Vonnie and Joe wandered around the neighborhood. Soon they found themselves at the entrance to Stonybrook Park.

"Let's walk beside the brook for a while," Joe suggested.

The sun was just setting. It was dark and cool under the trees overhanging the brook. Joe took Vonnie's hand.

"I'm glad you decided to send in the application," he said. "I care about you, you know."

"I know," Vonnie said. "And I care about you, too, Joe."

"Uh . . . I . . . I happened to make this for you today, after work," Joe said, reaching into his shirt pocket. What he pulled out had started as a steel welding rod. But a torch had melted and twisted it into the shape of a heart. Then Joe had hammered the heart until it looked lacy and ruffled.

"Joe!" Vonnie cried. "You made this for me?"

"Well," he said, a little embarrassed. "You'll probably make better ones once you learn more about welding."

   "Thanks to you—and the chance you gave me," Vonnie said. "The chance of a lifetime!"

   Vonnie threw her arms around Joe and kissed him. She had learned that when your chance comes along, you should grab it with all your strength.